PRAISE FOR RABBI DR. SHMUL

"The Jewish mystical tradition teaches us that there is a co[nnection between tikkun olam--healing] the world--and *tikkun ha'lev*--healing ourselves. Recogniz[ing that the reality of brokenness of the] outer world is a manifestation of the state of our own inner worlds, we are invited to turn inwards and seek a deeper connection to self. This is not an act of narcissism or selfishness; on the contrary, we are invited to engage in this work out of the recognition that when we are more centered in purpose and connected to spirit, we grow our capacity to powerfully serve others. In this book, Rabbi Yanklowitz offers you an invitation to turn inwards. I encourage you to accept the invitation; it is a sacred gift of guidance along the path towards spiritual growth from one of the brightest Jewish lights of our time."

- Dr. Max Klau - Developmental Psychologist, Leadership Scholar and Consultant

"The soul ceaselessly yearns for pathways of expression. Many humans suffer great emotional and physical pain which stems from a block of authentic expression. This book is an aid in the revelation of our essence. This book is a sacred tool in discerning our unique souls purpose for being embodied. It poses sacred questions which inevitably lead to sacred answers."

- Reb Pesach Stadlin - Eden Village Camp: Director of Jewish Living & Elijah Interfaith Institute: Project Manager

"Journal writing is a powerful practice for spiritual growth. But let's face it, many people struggle with this discipline. With this book, Rav Shmuly offers a real gift to the experienced practitioner and the novice alike. He offers practical and inspiring guidance for awakening the soul through the written word. I look forward to using the prompts in my own practice and recommend them to anyone on a path of spiritual growth."

- Rabbi David Jaffe – Founder, The Kirva Institute

"*Cheshbon hanefesh*, taking stock of our life, can help us live in better alignment with our most cherished values and with greater wisdom. Using the prompts in this book as a way to engage in this *cheshbon hanefesh* will be particularly helpful because committing pen to paper refines the quality of reflecting. It will give the seeker/writer the opportunity to clarify and focus his or her thinking, allowing realization of half-recognized truths in a fresh way. This opens all kinds of new opportunities for living a more awake life."

- Rabbi Lisa L. Goldstein - Institute for Jewish Spirituality, Executive Director

"Torah and tradition call on us to make ourselves into holy vessels. Intellectual endeavor alone can't bring about that transformation — we also need practices that touch and transform the heart. In "Soul Searching," R' Shmuly has provided valuable and accessible practical guidance that will help you search the hidden chambers of your inner world. Follow these sign posts and you will craft a new you, worthy of being called "a candle of God" (Mishlei 20:27)."

- Dr. Alan Morinis - Dean, The Mussar Institute

SOUL SEARCHING

A Jewish Workbook for Spiritual Exploration and Growth

Rabbi Dr. Shmuly Yanklowitz

© 2014

"I want to write, but more than that, I want to bring out all kinds of things that lie buried in my heart."

– Anne Frank, *The Diary of a Young Girl*

This book is dedicated to my Creator.

God - only You hold the true and perfect knowledge of my soul, my potential, and my destiny.

May You bring me closer so that I may actualize Your unique plans for me.

May our writing bring us into your intimate den where we may study Your/our soul together with You. Through our partnership, let us have the wherewithal to repair souls and the world together.

Contents and Writing Exercises

Introduction and Acknowledgments
Preparatory Considerations Before Beginning Spiritual Writing

Daily Living

Gratitude	~	22
Intellectual Growth	~	24
Life Priorities	~	26
Daily Rhythm	~	28
Inspiration	~	30
Meaning of Life	~	32
Work	~	34
Making a Big Decision	~	36
Mastering Our Short Game	~	38
Spiritual Seeking	~	40
Open To God's Plan	~	42
Organizing Your Theology Part I	~	44
Time Management	~	46
Life Essentials	~	48
Who Am I?	~	50
Organizing Your Theology Part II	~	52
Before Sleep	~	54
Dream Interpretation	~	56
Waking	~	58
Life Mission Statement	~	60

Joyous Occasions

Birthday	~	64
Anniversary	~	66
Expecting a Baby	~	68
Birth	~	70
Birth Celebrations	~	72
Bar and Bat Mitzvah	~	74
Graduation	~	76
Wedding	~	78
Job Promotion	~	80

Loss

End of Life	~	84
In Our Last Moments	~	86
Death	~	88
The Bereaved	~	90
End of a Relationship	~	92
When You're Feeling Down	~	94
Leaving a Job	~	96

Regrets	৵	98
Divorce	৵	100
Shame	৵	102

Social Change

Taking on a New Issue	৵	106
Striving Amidst Diversity	৵	108
Environment	৵	110
Animals	৵	112
Food	৵	114
Finding Your Cause	৵	116
Gates of Heaven Part I	৵	118
Gates of Heaven Part II	৵	120

Social Justice

Invisible People	৵	124
Idolatry	৵	126
Holy Chutzpah	৵	128
Protest Against Poverty	৵	130

Middot and Mitzvot

Your Best Self	৵	134
Losing Control	৵	136
Thirteen Attributes of Mercy	৵	138
Middot Exercise	৵	140
Mitzvot	৵	144
Your Unique *Mitzvah*	৵	146
Acts of Kindness	৵	148
Merciful, Modest and Kind	৵	150
Love All Around	৵	152
Activities That Matter	৵	154
Tochecha	৵	156
Loving Others	৵	158
On One Foot	৵	160
Daily Kindness	৵	162

Virtues

Beauty	৵	166
The Light Within Us	৵	168
Measured Disposition	৵	170
Seeing Our Full Selves	৵	172
Truth and Kindness	৵	174
Busy With Good	৵	176
Yetzer Hara vs. *Yetzer Tov*	৵	178
Using Your Power	৵	180

Leadership

Leadership	184
Role of a Jewish Leader	186
Moral Development	188
Optimism	190
Courage	192
Self-Inspiration	194
Productive Jealousy	196
Productive Agitation	198
Leadership Challenges	200
Blind Spots	202
The Balcony and the Dance Floor	204

Imagination

Camera Crew	208
Eternal Recurrence	210
Newspaper Headlines	212
Winning the Lottery	214
Job Interview	216
Writing a Letter	218

Happiness and Spirituality

Joyful Living	222
Radical Amazement	224
Opening your Heart	226
Positive Energy	228
Four-Fold Song	230
The Spoken Word	232
Self-Care Part I	234
Silence	236
The Accomplishments Within You	238
And Now What?	240

Relationships

People You Love	244
Community Part I	246
Teachers and Mentors	248
Students and Teachers	250
Friendship	252
Trust	254
Toxic Forces	256
Fear of Social Alienation	258
Community Part II	260
Jews and Gentiles	262
Role Models	264

Healing

Regret	ઔ	268
Self-Care Part II	ઔ	270
Wronged	ઔ	272
Physical Health	ઔ	274
Fear	ઔ	276

Prayer and Ritual

Prayer	ઔ	280
Cultivating the Soul	ઔ	282
Singing	ઔ	284
Features of the Jewish Tradition	ઔ	286
Reverence for Creation	ઔ	288
Conversion	ઔ	290

Journeying

Preparing for a Trip	ઔ	294
End of a Life Journey or Stage	ઔ	296
Legacy	ઔ	298
Retirement	ઔ	300

Growth

Freedom	ઔ	304
Obstacles	ઔ	306
Argument	ઔ	308
Your Well	ઔ	310
Measuring Success	ઔ	312
Struggle	ઔ	314
Blinders	ઔ	316
Moral Inconsistency	ઔ	318
Getting Back Up	ઔ	320
Theory of Behavioral Modification	ઔ	322
Vision	ઔ	324
Momentum	ઔ	326
Sacrifice	ઔ	328
Life Curriculum	ઔ	330
Daily Tasks to Improve	ઔ	332
Striving For Excellence	ઔ	334

Reflecting on the Past

Learning Moments	ઔ	338
Traumas and Glories	ઔ	340
Childhood	ઔ	342
Nostalgia	ઔ	344

Yichus	~	346
Ethical Dilemmas	~	348

Morning Blessings

Day and Night	~	352
Sight to the Blind	~	354
Clothes the Naked	~	356
Releases the Bound	~	358
Straightens the Bent	~	360
Strength to the Weary	~	362
Gives Knowledge	~	364

Ethics of the Fathers

World Stands on Three Things	~	368
Motivation	~	370
Sages	~	372
Relationships	~	374
Peace	~	376
Myself and Others	~	378
Greeting Others	~	380
Law, Truth, and Peace	~	382
Community Part III	~	384
Study	~	386
Good Traits	~	388
Overcoming Negativity	~	390
Property of Others	~	392
Work	~	394
Resiliency	~	396
Fear of Doing Wrong	~	398
Deeds Before Wisdom	~	400
Supporting Leaders	~	402
Humility	~	404
Afterlife	~	406
Beyond the Surface	~	408
Rechanneling Energy	~	410
Temperaments	~	412
Learning and Filtering	~	414
Love	~	416
Disputes	~	418

Inspirational Quotes

Great Transformations	~	422
Paradox	~	424
Become a Self	~	426
I Control My Life	~	428
Our Thoughts	~	430
Solitude	~	432

Boundaries	✍	434
Transitions	✍	436
Wasting Your Spiritual Capital	✍	438
Concern For Others	✍	440
The Law of Giving	✍	442
Flow	✍	444
Spiritual Being	✍	446
Going Inward	✍	448
Meaning	✍	450
Emotional Intelligence	✍	452
Habits of the Mind	✍	454
Our Grand Spectacle	✍	456
Responsible for Oneself	✍	458
Raise Your Standards	✍	460
Going Out To The Woods	✍	462
Building Castles In The Sky	✍	464
How You Make Others Feel	✍	466

Meditation and Writing

Fun	✍	470
Each Moment	✍	472
Standing Up	✍	474
Wearing Our Own Clothes	✍	476
Peace Through Conflict	✍	478
Ethical Will	✍	480
Meditation	✍	482
Mental States	✍	484
Channeling Emotions	✍	486
Divine Chariot	✍	488
Hitbodedut and *Hitbonenut*	✍	490
Self-Understanding	✍	492
Writing A Prayer	✍	494
Wonder	✍	496
Missing the Burning Bush	✍	498
Standing Before The Divine	✍	500
Your Inner Light	✍	502
Sefirot	✍	504

Holidays

Rosh Hashanah	✍	508
Yom Kippur	✍	510
Sukkot	✍	512
Simchat Torah	✍	514
Chanukah	✍	516
Tu B'Shevat	✍	518
Purim	✍	520
Passover	✍	522
Counting the Omer	✍	524

Yom HaShoah	≈	528
Yom Ha'Atzmaut	≈	530
Lag B'Omer	≈	532
Shavuot	≈	534
Tisha B'Av	≈	536
Shabbat	≈	538
Minor Fast Days	≈	540

Conclusion

Introduction and Acknowledgments

I wish someone gave me a workbook years ago. For the last two decades, I have been on an introspective journey to understand myself, my feelings, my responsibilities, my relationships, and my growth as a human being. This journey has been explored through conversations, writing, prayer, and meditation. I have come to believe that God has placed answers inside of us. We just need the time, space, inspiration and tools to access those pearls of wisdom.

I was always writing as a child: writing notes, writing stories, writing thoughts. It wasn't until my senior year of high school, though, that I began to finally personalize those thoughts in a more structured and reflective way. I am very thankful for Mr. White and Ms. Foucault who taught my Honors Literature and History course where they taught me to free-write for the first time. This was an incredibly rich daily experience of reflecting and writing after being presented specific prompts.

It was during my travels overseas to dozens of countries where I first put this skill into action. My writing prompts and questions were always very simple (as they are in this book) as they were about and concerned with big questions. I began to reflect more deeply with the pen than I ever had before.

My dear friend and mentor, Dr. Max Klau, created "The Idealist Journey," a curriculum that has inspired thoughtful intellectual and spiritually introspective work used to enhance leadership. I am grateful for what I learned at Wexner and Selah leadership trainings. I learned quite a bit from Professor Bob Kegan while I was at Harvard University studying in Adult Development. Furthermore, a key part of my Columbia University doctoral dissertation work was observing how prompted writing enhances one's meta-cognition.

I began implementing these tools as a leader of Jewish service learning programs for the American Jewish World Service, Panim, and Uri L'Tzedek. I used prompted writings for students to foster their leadership and inner worlds; I grew immensely along with my students.

In rabbinical school, I started to write passionately and consistently. I began to go deeper into my own feelings and spiritual quests. I am thankful to Ms. Merle Feld who continued a journey of spiritual writing with me throughout rabbinical school and to Yeshivat Chovevei Torah who supported this exploration. That special place that Merle held for us was a gift. Merle is a writer, poet, and spiritual guide, a great teacher.

I would also like to thank Abraham J. Frost for his superb editorial input for this workbook. His steady commitment and long hours with the project have been enormously helpful.

The most intense writing experience of my life was during my doctoral dissertation. While this writing was less personally reflective, there was constant demand to move forward. I learned perseverance and how to break through ideas to reach new paradigms like I never had before. My dissertation advisor, Dr. Deanna Kuhn, was a strong mentor and coach who helped me improve my writing.

My most personal and meaningful spiritual journey has been with Shoshana, my dear life partner. *Shoshanat Yaakov tzahala v'samaicha* (The rose of the Jewish people is full of joy and exultation). My dear Shoshana is a source of light and joy for all who encounter her and I am so deeply grateful. Our sweet daughter, Amiella Rachel, continues to teach me how to see the world through fresh eyes of wonder and amazement.

My writing helped me to answer questions, to handle loss and transition, to give me strength, to search for higher purpose, to grow, and so much more. Since I have gained so much from writing in ways that I could never have imagined, I decided I wanted to share this gift with others.

I intend for writers to use this book for at least a year, practicing the art of spiritual writing. Some exercises are reserved for special occasions (times of joy or loss, for example) while others can be taken up and completed at any time. One needs their own psychological and spiritual tools to succeed at fully exploring these prompts. The prompts are often deliberately vague and do not provide the tools for how each person should approach the question; that is left for the individual to decide. The reason for this is to honor the diversity of spiritual seekers and to embrace openly the very subjective prompts while exploring them as much as possible.

Reflective practices are more important today than they ever have been in the past. As society moves faster, we must have spaces where we move at a slower pace, giving us the opportunity to make sense of ourselves and the world. Writing can be an integral part of the slowing down and reflecting process that assists us in ensuring that we become who we need to be.

May our writing reveal deep insights that help us to grow and actualize our life potential.

Preparatory Considerations Before Beginning Spiritual Writing

As you consider your writing, attempt to answer these practical questions:

- Where is the place that will be most optimal for your growth as a writer? Which place will you sit in when you write that will enable you to go to a deeper place? A private room? A coffee shop? A library?

- Do you want silence? Light music? Solitude?

- Where can you find the right body posture to ensure you're comfortable?

- What would be special to have with you? A special chair? Blanket? Tea?

- How will you turn off other distractions (conversations, phones, computers)?

- Would it help you to have a writing partner? Or a writing group?

- How will you time your journal writing to ensure you have a set start and finish time? How will you add it to your daily or weekly calendar?

- What ritual can you engage to tap into a deeper place before you begin?

- Can you consider meditating before and after your writing sessions? What types of meditations will most help to clear your mind and enhance your reflective experience?

- Can you steady your breathing and focus your thinking before beginning?

- What closing ritual can you engage to transition from the emotional state reached in your writing back to your normal day?

- How will you avoid writing only when in one particular mood (whether good or bad)?

Don't worry about grammar or spelling or about making sense to anyone else. The goal is not to be the greatest writer, but about to access your innermost thoughts. It is okay to contradict yourself and not to make total sense. In fact, it's essential to gaining clarity. There are a few writing sections that might not apply to you at this stage of your life (retirement or having a baby, etc.) but the majority of the prompts can be filled out by anyone regardless of age, gender, denomination, belief, or ideology.

I have intentionally left a lot of blank space for your writing. I have found that structure is really important for spiritual writing (a set time to write, a set place to write, a set amount of space to write in, etc.). It is easy to slide with spiritual practices and structure helps to solidify and reinforce commitment. I encourage you to start writing in this book since it is a very accessible way to begin. It will also make it easy to go back to read all of your collective entries. We will all have different needs regarding structure vs. autonomy and we should explore what works best for each of us. Happy writing!

Daily Living

Gratitude

What do you feel most grateful for? Make a list.

How can you cultivate more gratitude into your daily living? How can you express your appreciation and gratitude more fully?

Intellectual Growth

How are you challenging yourself on a day-to-day basis?

What new activities can you start to continue to grow intellectually (reading, writing, classes, etc.)?

Life Priorities

What are the key 3-5 life priorities you have that you want to keep on the center of your mind throughout your daily living?

How can you set up reminders to ensure that you're consistently focused on these priorities?

Daily Rhythm

Sometimes very small changes can make very big differences. For example, the Greek philosopher Pythagoras brought forth the idea that musical notes are created by differing lengths of string (like musical notes made by striking anvils of varying size).

Is there subtle music you can hear and play that exists in the nuanced areas of your life? Are there some minor adjustments you can make to your daily rhythm?

Inspiration

What inspires you? Make a list.

How can you connect more deeply with your inspiration to ensure your fire is lit?

Meaning of Life

Viktor Frankl, Holocaust survivor, psychiatrist, and preeminent existential philosopher, taught that the question is not "what is the meaning of life," but "what is the meaning of your life?"

How would you answer this question? What is the core meaning in your life that keeps you going?

Work

For many, work is a very meaningful part of life. For others, it's a challenging break from a real, actualized life. Either way, it is the way we spend the bulk of our lives.

How can you add more meaning into your workday (improving relationships at work, beautifying your work space, how you use your break time, etc.)?

Making a Big Decision

What is a big decision you're trying to make right now?

How can you slow down to be really intentional with this decision?

Who are your partners that you can talk through the issue with?

Mastering Our Short Game

Marshall Goldsmith, a prominent author and motivational speaker, writes about making small changes in our life via a poignant golf analogy:

> "In a way, I can see why people have problems choosing what needs fixing. In golf, for example, it is common wisdom that 70 percent of all shots take place within 100 yards of the pin. It's called the short game, and it involves pitching, chipping, hitting out of sand traps, and putting. If you want to lower your score, focus on fixing your short game: it represents at least 70 percent of your score. Yet, if you go to a golf course you'll see very few people practicing their short game. They're all at the driving range trying to hit their oversized drivers as far as they can. Statistically, it doesn't make sense because over the course of eighteen holes, they'll only need their drivers fourteen times (at most) whereas they'll pull out their short irons and putters at least fifty times. Athletically it does not make sense either. The short game demands compact delicate small-muscle movements; it is much easier to master than the violent big-muscle movements of driving off the tee. Nor does it make sense competitively. If you improve your short game, you will shoot lower scores-and beat the competition," (*What Got You Here Won't Get You There*, 186).

We often look at big problems and challenges while glossing over the more day-to-day issues that we can address in our lives. What is the short game you're glossing over in your life?

Spiritual Seeking

Too often, we find ourselves stuck and complacent in our spiritual lives doing the same spiritual practices with the same intentions. Over time, these rituals inevitably become rote and less meaningful.

How can you search more deeply? What would you like to be more connected to?

Open to God's Plan

Do you keep windows open in your life for God to intervene or do you keep tight control of everything?

Are there some spaces you can leave more open for someone to engage you, for something to catch your eye, for some place to grab you?

How do you balance control with being receptive to an outside intervention into your life?

Organizing Your Theology Part I

What do you believe about the creation of the universe?

What do you believe about revelation?

What are your beliefs around prophecy?

What do you believe about miracles and Divine intervention?

What do you believe about the messianic era?

What do you believe about the afterlife?

How can you continue to learn more to get clarity on your beliefs?

Time Management

Make a chart and track how you use your hours in the coming week (all 24 hours for 7 days). Then add up the hours you spend in each activity (work, sleep, exercise, entertainment, eating, etc.). Then, make a list of your core life priorities and compare that list to your previous time allocation list.

How can your time allocation become aligned with your life goals?

What skills of time management do you need to learn and where can you go for those?

How can you squeeze in more activities that are "important" (visioning, preparation, learning, self-care, etc), but not urgent (crisis, deadlines, consistent problems)?

Life Essentials

What are your real life essentials? What do you need and can not live without? What are wants and desires in your life that you could live without?

Do your needs and wants ever conflict? Do your needs and wants ever conflict with the needs and wants of others at home or work?

How do you navigate these tensions?

Who Am I?

Rabbi Menachem Mendel of Kotzk once said: "If I am I because you are you, and you are you because I am I, then I am not I and you are not you. But if I am I because I am I, and you are you because you are you, then I am I and you are you."

We often get stuck defining ourselves relative to others but this is not truly us, just a false perception.

Who are you?

What is your unique essence, your unique story? What are you all about?

Organizing Your Theology Part II

Where are you willing to hold on to ambiguity and uncertainty?

Can you remain committed to Judaism without having perfect answers to these great timeless questions?

How might your practices change based upon your beliefs?

Where are a few places you can read more about the issues you are struggling with?

Before Sleep

There is a Jewish ritual before sleep to pray for good dreams. Below is the text translated in English:

"Blessed are You Hashem our God, King of the Universe Who casts the bonds of sleep upon my eyes and slumber upon my eyelids. May it be Your will, Hashem my God and the God of my forefathers, that You lay me down to sleep in peace and raise me up in peace. May I not be confounded by my ideas, dreams that are bad and fleeting thoughts that are bad, may my offspring be perfect before You, and may You illuminate my eyes lest I [die in sleep], for it is You who illuminates the pupil of the eye. Blessed are you Hashem, Who illuminates the entire world with Your glory."

How can you embrace your final minutes before sleep to cultivate the right mental state for the coming hours?

Dream Interpretation

The Talmud teaches, "All dreams follow the mouth" (*Brachot* 56). That is to say that our dreams only take on the reality we give them.

The truth of a dream is determined by our interpretation of it. How are you actively interpreting your dreams in a way that is strengthening you?

Write about 3 of the last dreams you can recall and actively interpret them in a way that is positive.

Waking

מוֹדֶה אֲנִי לְפָנֶיךָ, מֶלֶךְ חַי וְקַיָּם, שֶׁהֶחֱזַרְתָּ
בִּי נִשְׁמָתִי בְּחֶמְלָה; רַבָּה אֱמוּנָתֶךָ.

There is a Jewish ritual (*Modeh ani*) to express gratitude upon waking up. The Talmud teaches that we die a little bit in our sleep and that God gives us a vote of confidence when we wake (giving us new life and purpose).

How can you embrace a waking ritual that helps to fill you with gratitude and purpose each morning?

Life Mission Statement

Organizations have mission statements, an ethos. We need them for our lives as well.

Write your life mission statement. It should only be 4-6 sentences and encapsulate what you are about and how you are committed to living.

Joyous Occasions

Birthday

How are you feeling about your upcoming birthday? How can this birthday start a new year where you live more like your ideal self?

What can be improved in your life?

Anniversary

On a wedding or dating anniversary, write about all the things you love about your partner.

How can you focus more on these things you love than on the aspects you might find more challenging? How can you express more often how much you love these traits and deeds of your partner?

Write about ways you can show more love to your life-partner.

Expecting a Baby

How are you feeling about the arrival of your baby?

What values will determine what name you give him/her? What dreams do you have for him/her? What fears do you have as a parent?

Who are your partners in this journey?

How are you preparing to embrace this challenge?

Birth

How are you expressing gratitude for this miraculous birth?

Write about the baby you love that was just born. What do you wish for him/her? How will you support this child in his/her life journey?

Birth Celebrations

(If you had a baby boy, reflect on the prompt regarding *brit milah*. If you had a baby girl, reflect on the prompt regarding *simchat bat*).

Brit Milah (*bris*) – Through this ceremony on the eighth day of life (conditions permitting), a baby boy enters the Jewish covenant just as Abraham did 4,000 years ago. God partners with humans to complete creation. The Chassidic masters teach that at the cry of a baby at a *brit*, the heavens are compassionately open for our prayers. It is considered a very sacred moment, not merely a health-based procedure of circumcision.

How can this ceremony be made most meaningful for you and your family? What goes through your mind at the thought of going through one of these ceremonies?

Simchat Bat – At a simchat bat, the baby girl is celebrated and named. This ritual is an anomaly—unlike most other rituals, the simchat bat has no strict ancient tradition, and thus there is tremendous room for creativity at this ceremony. Thus, the parents have room to create their own tradition in welcoming their baby girl into the world.

How can this ceremony be made most meaningful for you and your family? What goes through your mind at the thought of going through one of these ceremonies?

Bar and Bat Mitzvah

Consider this prompt before someone close to you is having his or her bar/bat mitzvah:

It is only in a limited sense that when a 13-year-old Jewish boy and a 12-year-old Jewish girl become "adults." Developmental psychologists actually now suggest that "emerging adulthood" occurs even later than previously anticipated, at 18-26 years old.

Rather, a bar or bat mitzvah (son/daughter of responsibility) are considered "adults" in the eyes of tradition. The core years of Jewish obligation and influence that their parents desperately embraced are now over. The adolescent is now expected to evolve from extrinsic motivations (incentives and rewards) toward intrinsic motivations (goodness, holiness, and justness). While one has not embraced any true milestones of adulthood such as having a full-time job, marriage, raising children, meeting financial responsibilities, etc., he or she is now responsible for having an impact upon the Jewish people and broader society.

How did your bar/bat mitzvah affect you? Did you grow in your commitment to the Jewish community?

What wishes do you have for the bar/bat mitzvah adolescent you're preparing, supporting, and celebrating?

If you never had the ceremony, might you consider doing it as an adult?

Graduation

Consider all the steps you had to take to get here.

What does graduation day mean to you? What will you do with the knowledge you have gained while pursuing your degree?

Who helped you succeed? Who do you have to personally thank?

Wedding

A wedding is one of the most powerful Jewish rituals. Having led many, there are few that I myself don't tear up at. A Jewish wedding is a celebration of a contractual agreement towards shared obligation, responsibility, and respect. Love is made concrete into committed action, making a wedding another way to remind us that while our marriages and families are inherently valuable, they can also be vehicles toward enacting social justice and *tikkun olam* (repairing the world).

How may this upcoming wedding help to bring you closer to God and to those you love?

Job Promotion

Mazel tov!

How will you celebrate?

Who are some of the people in your life that support you that you want to thank?

How might you use any extra funding from your new position you might be receiving to give back to the community?

How might you use some increased power or opportunity to help others to rise up?

Loss

End of Life

What are you feeling as you prepare for this upcoming loss?

In addition to caring for a loved one, how are you caring for yourself at this time?

How can you leave a bit more time and space in your life to process, grieve, and mourn?

In Our Last Moments

The rabbis taught that King David was afraid of his death and so he inquired with God as to when he would die. God responded that his last day would be on a Shabbat, a day of rest. From that point on, David spent every Shabbat, both day and night, in deep Torah study. When the day of his death arrived, the Angel of Death saw that David was in deep study and meditation. His virtue overpowered the Angel of Death.

What action do you want to be found doing when you're time to pass arrives?

How will you make sure you are immersed in that action?

Death

What practice of mourning can you embrace to honor the memory of your loved one and to enter a journey of healing for yourself? What good deeds can you do in his/her memory?

What were some of the little things about this individual that you (will) sorely miss?

The Bereaved

Rabbi David Hartman once said: "When should a rabbi visit the bereaved? On the eighth day."

Typically mourners are visited during *shiva* (the first seven days after burial). The suggestion here is that we should not leave mourners alone and be just as committed (if not more) after their *shiva* ends.

What is a practice you can adopt for comforting, supporting, or visiting those who are in periods of bereavement and loss?

End of a Relationship

What are some aspects of this person you will miss? What are aspects you will not miss?

How can you find others in your life that you can share love with?

When You're Feeling Down

What has brought you down today? Is this something unique today that you can address? If so, how can you address this issue? If this is more chronic, what is the deeper challenge and its origin in your life?

What are 2-3 actions you can take to bring yourself back up when you get down? What works for you?

Who can help to support this journey?

<u>Leaving a Job</u>

What will you miss about this job? What will you not miss?

How can you leave and transition with pride and honor? What will be next on your journey?

Regrets

If you were to die tomorrow, God forbid, what would you regret not having done with your life?

Write about what matters most to you. Also write about the activities that you don't do enough. What things do you value you may have never done?

Divorce

While a divorce is innately a tragic event (a relationship has broken and attempts at repair have failed), it can also be a liberating experience, perhaps even a source of relief and joy.

Why do you think divorce was the outcome of your relationship?

How did you get the support you needed (or how will you provide it to someone else who may be going through a divorce now)?

Shame

One of the most painful of human emotions is shame. There are many different manifestations of shame in the human experience as this emotion can be highly relative and personal.

How have you experienced shame in your life?

What defense mechanism do you tend to employ when you feel shame?

How can this negative reaction be transferred into a positive opportunity?

Social Change

Taking on a New Issue

In addition to all of the holy work you already do, what is one additional cause/project you can take on in the coming year to add more light in the world?

Striving Amidst Diversity

Consider this excerpt from the poem *If* by Rudyard Kipling:

"If you can dream – and not make dreams your master;
   If you can think – and not make thoughts your aim;
If you can meet with Triumph and Disaster
   And treat those two impostors just the same;
If you can bear to hear the truth you've spoken
   Twisted by knaves to make a trap for fools,
Or watch the things you gave your life to, broken,
   And stoop and build 'em up with worn-out tools"

How might you continue dreaming and striving amidst the challenges in your life? What are these main obstacles that you need to overcome?

Environment

What are you doing to help preserve the environment?

Who are some friends and mentors modeling environmental practices that you can learn more from?

<u>Animals</u>

There are many vulnerable animals in the world looking for protection.

How can you connect more with them?

Have you considered adopting a pet from a shelter?

How can you cut more meat out of your weekly diet?

Food

How can you become more reflective in your eating process? Consider some avenues for growth:

- Healthy eating
- *Kashrut*
- Blessings before and after food
- Labor practices
- Animal welfare
- Fair trade
- Environmental impact
- Local food

What are some baby steps you can make to transform your food consumption into a more spiritual and ethical practice?

Finding Your Cause

What keeps you up at night?

What is one issue that you need to see radically different in the world in ten years?

What cause are you willing to invest in and see to the end?

Gates of Heaven Part I

There is one profound (and haunting) question I believe will be asked of us at the Gates of Heaven: "Did you give more than you took from the world?"

Given our years of childhood, how much we consume as adults, and the predominant self-protection and self-serving culture we live in, few of us can honestly say that we've given the world more than we've taken.

How can you strive to get closer? Where can you reduce your taking and where can you increase your giving?

Gates of Heaven Part II

Rava (a sage in the Talmud) taught that at the Gates of Heaven, there are certain questions one will be asked (*Shabbat* 31a):

- Did you conduct your (business) affairs honestly?
- Did you set aside a special/regular time in your schedule for Torah study?
- Did you do all you could to have children?
- Did you yearn for world redemption?
- Did you deal deeply in matters of wisdom?
- Did you learn critically?
- But even if you did this, it is of limited value in comparison to the value that if fear of God was in a person's storage-house, then yes (this individual's judgment is favorable). If not, then no (it is not favorable).

How would you respond to each of these seven questions?

Which question do you think will be primarily relevant for your life?

Social Justice

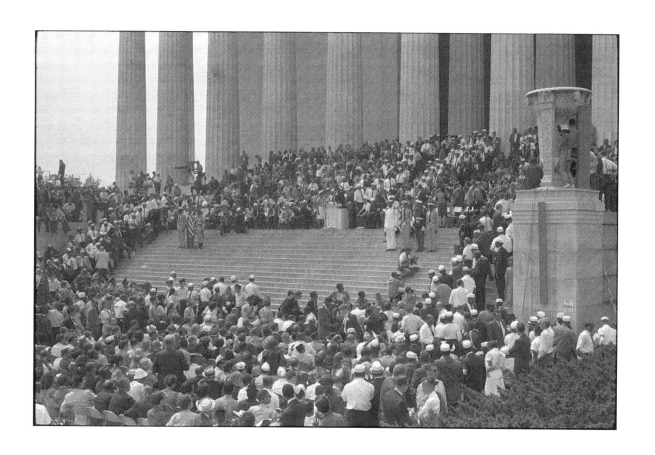

Invisible People

There are many invisible people in society that are neither seen nor heard. Yet, they live among us, use the same public resources we do, and have the same wants and desire as any other person.

Who are at least three invisible people you know that you can give voice and sight to?

Idolatry

The rabbis taught, "All those who deny idolatry are called a Jew" (*Megillah* 13a).

Few of us today are drawn toward worshipping stars or statues but the desire for idolatry is still alive.

What are some things (other than God) that you give absolute significance to (money, image, career, etc.) to the point where one could claim you "worship" it?

How can you break your dependence on this false worship?

Holy Chutzpah

Our forefather Abraham challenged God to understand the meaning of justice. The rabbis called this *hutzpah kelapei shemaya* (audacity towards heaven).

Where do you have questions, concerns, or complaints toward heaven that you might productively raise?

Protest Against Poverty

The rabbis believed poverty was an unmatched tragedy. They taught in a Midrash (*Exodus Rabbah* 31:14):

> "Nothing in the universe is worse than poverty; it is the most terrible of sufferings. A person oppressed by poverty is like someone who carried on his shoulders the weight of the whole world's sufferings. If all the pain and all the suffering of this world were placed on one scale and poverty on the other, the balance would tilt towards poverty."

What is your protest against poverty? What small dent might you make to release others from poverty?

Middot and *Mitzvot*

Your Best Self

Consider a time when you were pleased with yourself.

Describe what it felt like and what it was really about for you.

What side of you emerged and how can you cultivate that more deeply?

Losing Control

Jewish tradition teaches that once one has done something wrong three times, one has psychologically justified it being done. Further, the late Professor Nahum Sarna wrote:

> "The 'hardening of the heart' thus expresses a state of arrogant moral degeneracy, unresponsive to reason and incapable of compassion. Pharaoh's personal culpability is beyond question. It is to be noted that in the first five plagues Pharaoh's obduracy is self-willed. It is only thereafter that it is attributed to Divine causality. This is the biblical way of asserting that the king's intransigence has by then become habitual and irreversible; his character has become his destiny. He is deprived of the possibility of relenting and is irresistibly impelled to his self-wrought doom," (The JPS Torah Commentary of Exodus 21).

Once one has hardened one's heart enough, one may lose control of softening it. Where are you on the verge of losing control of yourself by building habits of the mind and heart that are so strong they may become irrevocable?

How can you regain some control before it is lost?

Thirteen Attributes of Mercy

The pinnacle of the *selichot* service (penitential prayers for forgiveness) is the *yud-gimel middot* (Thirteen Attributes of Mercy) where we recount God's merciful and compassionate ways. We seek to emulate these ways.

What are ways that you can cultivate different types of compassion? Compassion for family that may frustrate you at times? Compassion for someone struggling in your midst? Compassion for strangers? Compassion for animals?

Middot Development

Jewish Character Trait Development

Please rate yourself on a 1 – 10 scale (10-mastered this trait, 1-struggle very much with this trait)

1. Humility - *Anivut* _____
2. Patience - *Savlanut* _____
3. Gratitude - *Hakarat Hatov* _____
4. Compassion - *Rachamim* _____
5. Honor - *Kavod* _____
6. Enthusiasm/Joy - *Simcha* _____
7. Speech - *Shmirat Halashon* _____
8. Truth - *Emet* _____
9. Judge Favorably - *Dan L'chaf zechut* _____
10. Open-minded, tolerant - *Sovlanut* _____
11. Loving-Kindness - *Chesed – Ahava* _____
12. Responsibility - *Acharayut* _____
13. Commitment - *Neemanut* _____
14. Honesty - *Yashar* _____
15. Sensitive - *Regishut* _____
16. Slow to Anger - *Erech Hapaiim* _____
17. Zeal/Alacrity - *Zerizut* _____
18. Careful - *Hakpadot* _____
19. Peace-Making - *Rodef Shalom* _____
20. Cool headedness/Equanimity - *Menuchat Ha'Nefesh* _____

Now we will analyze two of the *middot* that we struggle most with:[1]

---

[1] This approach was introduced to me by Robert Kegan, The William and Miriam Meehan Professor in Adult Learning and Professional Development Educational Chair at the Harvard Graduate School of Education

1.) Write a character trait from the list provided above that you would like to work on:

_____

A. What are you doing (or not doing) that prevents you from growing in this trait:

_____

_____

B. What is your hidden commitment? What is at stake for you to change A? What is the "big thing" that you would have to give up (part of identity, pleasure, time, other priority)?

_____

_____

C. What's the big assumption (or commitment) that you hold that may need altering (the deeper place where B originated for you)?

_____

_____

D. What are 2-3 small steps that you can take to grow in this character trait (to address A and C):

_____

_____

2.) Write a character trait from the list provided above that you would like to work on:

_____

A. What are you doing (or not doing) that prevents you from growing in this trait:

_____

_____

B. What is your hidden commitment? What is at stake for you to change A? What is the "big thing" that you would have to give up (part of identity, pleasure, time, other priority)?

_____

_____

C. What's the big assumption (or commitment) that you hold that may need altering (the deeper place where B originated for you)?

_____

_____

D. What are 2-3 small steps that you can take to grow in this character trait (to address A and C):

_____

_____

Example Problem: <u>Impatience</u>

A. Get frustrated when someone wants to talk to me for longer than I have time for
B. Complete autonomy of my time, Self-centeredness, Lack of value for other
C. In my moments of impatience, I truly don't value the other person enough to just listen (must feel that my time is more valuable then their time is)
D. Leave more room in my agenda, Realize that their time is as important as mine, see how often I take the time of others.

Mitzvot

What are some particular *mitzvot* you wish to cultivate more deeply (quantitatively or qualitatively)? Make a list.

How might you grow in making these spiritual practices more meaningful, intentional, and transformative?

Your Unique *Mitzvah*

The Mei HaShiloach (Mordechai Yosef Leiner) taught that people have a particular *mitzvah* that is attached to their soul. He explains that this is why one has been created (to actualize this unique *mitzvah*).

What might your special mitzvah be that you will spend your life beautifying?

What do you think you might be created uniquely to do?

Acts of Kindness

The rabbis taught that "The following are the activities for which a person is rewarded in this world, and again in the World-to-Come: honoring one's father and mother, deeds of loving-kindness, and making peace between a person and his neighbor. The study of Torah, however, is as important as all of them together" (*Peah* 1:1).

Work through each of these four categories of commitment: honoring your parents, loving-kindness, being a broker of peace, and studying Torah.

How can you grow in each?

Merciful, Modest, and Kind

The rabbis taught: "The (Jewish) nation is distinguished by three characteristics; they are merciful, they are modest… and they perform acts of loving-kindness" (*Yevamot* 79a).

The rabbis teach that a Jew's highest aspirations are to be full of mercy, modesty, and kindness. How can you embrace each precept more deeply?

Love All Around

Arizal (Rabbi Isaac Luria) taught that before a person recites the Shema (foundational Jewish affirmation of faith), one should look and feel love for those around us; we cannot ask God for love if we ourselves do not feel love for others.

Try this experiment when you're sitting in a room full of people and try to fill yourself with love for them. Just sit with that feeling and hold onto it for some moments.

Write about your experience.

Activities that Matter

What are three or four very valuable acts that you did today?

How can you ensure that there are actions that you find innately valuable that you do every day?

Tochecha

There is a mitzvah to give *tochecha* (moral rebuke/feedback) when someone has erred. The rabbis teach today that most are not on a high enough spiritual level though to receive rebuke and that giving it to one who cannot hear it will only have a negative impact.

We all make spiritual and moral mistakes and miss our potentials. If we truly want to actualize ourselves, we must be open to having support and challenge to get there

Who are individuals in your life who you feel are spiritually receptive to hear feedback that you can support?

How can you become more reflective and open to receiving feedback from others?

Loving Others

The Torah teaches: "Love your neighbor as yourself" (Leviticus 19:18). The rabbis went further by teaching that this is the major principle of Torah (*Yerushalmi Nedarim* 9:4).

Bracketing family and close friends, how you experience love for your "neighbor?" How does self-love affect your neighbor-love?

What would your interactions with your "neighbors" look like if you loved them?

On One Foot

In a famous Talmudic passage, an individual approaches two sages (Hillel and Shammai) and asks them to teach him the Torah while the sage stands on one foot.

What would your response be?

What do you believe is the essence of Judaism that you would share in that moment to inspire others?

Daily Kindness

How can you ensure that you do acts of kindness each day (even if they're small)?

What might these acts look like for you?

Can you add this to your calendar or agenda?

Virtues

Beauty

What does beauty mean to you?

How can you connect more with art and nature to cultivate a deeper connection to beauty?

How can you cultivate more beauty in your inner world?

The Light Within Us

The Alter Rebbe wrote that one process of *teshuva* (repentance) is to awaken the spark of God within us. We can feel joy at the immanence of the Divine but also pain that God must suffer by being within all of our mistakes and limitations. The most radical notion of this idea is that when we work on ourselves we can actually be focused on our love for the *Divine* that is within us.

Experiment with this idea. Meditate on the spark of eternity within you.

How can you serve that light to ensure it is more free, bright, and loved?

Measured Disposition

Think about the stimuli that cause you to have immediate negative reactions that may be destructive or that you are not proud of. Name them.

Next time, when one of these negative stimuli emerges, be aware of it, and try to refrain from having that typical immediate reaction. What alternative responses could you experiment with in that moment?

Seeing Our Full Selves

What is one thing that your co-workers or friends would praise you for? What is one thing that most co-workers would complain about you?

How can you improve this aspect of your work-self?

Truth and Kindness

The Rabbis taught a fascinating Midrash:

> Rav Shimon said: When God was about to create Adam, the ministering angles split into different groups, some saying not to create him and some saying to create him. This is what is referred to when it says, "Kindness and Truth have encountered each other; Righteousness and Peace have met." Kindness said, "Create him, for he bestows kindness." Truth said, "Don't create him for he is full of falsehood." What did God do? He took truth and cast it to the Earth, as it is written, "And You threw truth earthwards." The angels said to God, "Master of the Universe, why do You degrade Your precious seal [of Truth]?" [God responded] "Let Truth rise from the ground, as it says, 'Truth from the land will sprout.'"

Where and how do you affirm truth even when it's painful? Where and how do you affirm kindness and love even when it may seem contradictory to truth?

Busy With Good

Rabbi Menachem Mendel of Kotzk once said: "I do not want followers who are righteous, rather I want followers who are too busy doing good that they won't have time to do bad."

We all have negative inclinations to waste time and serve ourselves. We can never kill that inner desire but we can try to replace it with better activities.

How can you channel more of your energy to being "busy with the good?"

Yetzer Hara vs. *Yetzer Tov*

The Jewish tradition teaches that *yetzer hara* (our evil inclination) is always at war with our *yetzer tov* (good inclination).

How does your evil inclination attempt to pull you away from your potential?

What strategies might you employ to defeat those temptations that lead you to make the wrong spiritual or moral choices?

Using Your Power

The French philosopher Michel Foucault taught that power is multi-directional. Everyone holds power and these dynamics are interconnected. Many of us think of "power" as a dirty or negative word but it doesn't have to be. Power is something we all hold and that gives us the normative capability of creating change. We can develop healthy empowerment to create change and also healthy disempowerment (*tzimtzum*) to create space for (and the possibility to give power to) others. One of today's great tragedies is that many feel that they are not capable of creating change because they cannot see the power they actually hold.

Power is not a singular thing. There are many forms: personal power, collaborative power, position power, institutional power, cultural power, structural power, referred power, expert power, ideological power, obstructive power, and transcendent power.[2]

Consider the types of power you hold in your life that may give you a sense of stability, confidence, and personal gain. How can you use those power positions to help people in need and to elevate others?

---

[2] Adapted from a Selah Leadership training conference program.

Leadership

Leadership

How do you exercise your leadership?

What values guide the way you lead?

What style of leadership is most comfortable for you? How can you grow as a leader?

Role of a Jewish Leader

Rabbi Hayyim of Brisk was asked what the function of a rabbi was in a community. Without hesitation he replied, "To redress the grievances of those who are abandoned and alone, to protect the dignity of the poor, and to save the oppressed from the hands of the oppressor."

This certainly should be applied beyond just rabbis to all Jewish leaders.

How do you see these tasks as a part of your life mission? How do you protect those that are under your guidance or in your midst?

Moral Development

Lawrence Kohlberg, the founder of the modern field of moral development, suggested that there are six stages of moral development that humans can pass through. Here is a very abbreviated explanation of them. Each stage represents one's motive in a moral dilemma:

- Obedience and Punishment - How can I avoid punishment?
- Self-interest – What reward can I attain?
- Conformity – How can I abide by social norms to be a good boy/girl?
- Social Order – How can I obey the law?
- Social Contract – How can I fulfill my relationship duties?
- Universal Ethical Principles – What does my conscience say I must do?

Engage in some soul-searching and critical thinking around what factors determine your moral decisions.

Write about a few moral dilemmas you have been through recently. What drove your decision-making?

__Optimism__

Sadly, after only a few mistakes, traumas, and challenges, the best of us can start becoming pessimistic or cynical. Optimism keeps us alive enabling us to continue to dream, see new possibilities, and remain hopeful amidst adversity.

Where do you find it easiest to be optimistic in your life? Where do you struggle seeing the positive?

What mind exercise can you employ to strengthen your optimism muscle in an authentic and honest way?

Courage

Rabbi Yitz Greenberg teaches that the verse "You shall not tremble before any man, for the judgment is God's" (Deuteronomy 1:17) means that we must have the spiritual courage to lead as we see fit. Anyone who takes on moral leadership will inevitably receive push back when trying to create change. This is where he says *imo anochi b'tzara* comes in (that God suffers long with us).

How can you bring God's closeness and support more into your moral leadership?

Further, what examples can you think of regarding courageous actions by leaders? They could be figures from the past or people you admire who are living today.

Self-Inspiration

The first key to being able to inspire others to actually live our own lives with inspiration.

Are you inspired by what you do, by your own ideas or by your passions and commitments?

How can you live with more inspiration?

Productive Jealousy

There is a rabbinic saying *kinat sofrim tarbeh chochma* (jealousy among sages increases wisdom).

Who is someone you are jealous of in a constructive way? Why this person in particular?

How can you ensure that your jealousy is not destructive but makes you better?

Productive Agitation

Conflict and discomfort are not always bad.

What is one area where you can allow yourself to be more agitated and uncomfortable in order to learn more deeply?

Leadership Challenges

Ron Heifetz of the Harvard Kennedy School is a leading thinker concerning technical challenges (marketing, recruitment, etc.) vs. adaptive challenges (moving people, creating systemic change, altering realities, etc.).

Where do you engage in technical leadership and where do you engage in adaptive leadership?

How can you start to see (and help others to see) the deeper adaptive challenges hidden among a multitude of challenges?

Blind Spots

We all have blind spots where we cannot see our true selves or how others perceive our behavior.

Who are some of your partners at work and outside of work that help you see your blind spots?

Who are the people best equipped to give you feedback to help you learn about yourself and grow?

The Balcony and the Dance Floor

Heifetz further explains that we must see the biggest picture when we lead. Some are comfortable staying safe on the balcony watching the dance but never engaging in the dance. Others are constantly dancing on the dance floor but never go up to the balcony to see the bigger picture or see how the dance has evolved.

The epistemic challenge is to continue to dance while we continue to watch the evolving drama we're engaged in from the balcony.

How do you join the dance? What makes you take a break to see the dancers in action from the balcony?

Imagination

Camera Crew

Imagine you have a camera crew to make whatever film you want.

What story would you tell and why?

What is the untold story that you think is vital to be shown of the human condition or of contemporary issues?

Eternal Recurrence

The philosopher Friedrich Nietzsche had us imagine what our reaction would be if we were told that we were to relive our lives repeatedly for all time, and whether this would be heaven or hell based on the life we had lived, including all the choices we had made in life.

If you were to eternally live your current existence over and over would that be a positive or negative experience?

How could you shift to a live a life and make choices that you would affirm for eternity?

Newspaper Headlines

Flip through a newspaper reading the headlines for about five minutes.

What do you feel after you've flipped through the paper for those 5 minutes? How does reading the papers (or blogs) affect you daily?

How can you spiritually transition from your daily encounter with local, national, and global news each day back into your immediate reality without that emotional baggage?

Winning the Lottery

Try out this test for honing in on your life purpose.

If you won the lottery tomorrow and no longer needed to work or do any kind of chores, what would you continue to do anyways?

What is so core to you that you wouldn't give it up under any circumstances?

Job Interview

If you have a job interview coming up, use this space to brainstorm.

What aspects of yourself do you want to emphasize during your interview? What questions do you have for the people interviewing you?

How can you bring your best, most true, and confident self to this interview?

Writing a Letter

Write a letter that you do not plan to send. It should be to someone you have something important to share with (but that you cannot actually share with or don't want to share with).

Happiness and Spirituality

Joyful Living

What is something you have recently done that filled you with joy?

Why was it so joyful for you?

How can you incorporate more of this type of joyful living into your life?

Radical Amazement

Rabbi Abraham Joshua Heschel wrote that we should live our lives full of "radical amazement" (in awe of existence).

How can you slow down to focus on living to cultivate more experiences of radical amazement?

Opening Your Heart

How can you open your heart?

What is blocking it (metaphorically speaking)? Where did this block originate?

What is blocking you from feeling more empathy, love, and/or compassion?

Positive Energy

Can you think of three people you know who embody life and zest (real positive energy) that make you feel connected? What is it about them that enables them to do that?

When do you feel the most positive and the most connected?

What can you do daily to maintain that connection and energy?

Can you think of a person in whose presence you feel more spiritually drained? What can you do to either help them grow or at least to protect yourself from being affected?

Four-Fold Song

Rabbi Abraham Isaac HaCohen Kook taught that each person has four songs (*Orot Hakodesh*, Volume II, 458-459):

1. The song of one's own life
2. The song of one's own people
3. The song of humanity
4. The song of all of existence

How are you singing each of these songs? Can you identify each for you? What is the relationship between each of these songs for you?

How are you listening to the songs of others? Can you join a symphony where your song is authentic and you allow the songs of others to be authentically alive as well?

The Spoken Word

Rabbi Joseph Soloveitchik wrote:

> "I do not intend to suggest a new method of remedying the human situation which I am about to describe; neither do I believe that it can be remedied at all… All I want is to follow the advice given by Elihu, the son of Berachel of old, who said, "I will speak that I may find relief" [Job 32:20]; for there is a redemptive value quality for an agitated mind in the spoken word, and a tormented soul finds peace in confessing (*The Lonely Man of Faith*, 2)

Where does your soul long for expression (or confession, if you will)? Who are your partners in this spiritual endeavor?

Self-Care Part I

How do you nurture yourself to ensure that you are happy and that your fire is shining bright?

Who do you allow to show you care?

What kinds of additional practices could you embrace to take care of yourself?

Silence

Close your eyes and sit in absolute silence for a period of time (5, 10, 20 minutes, etc.) and focus on the silence.

After that reflect: What did you "hear" in the silence? What thoughts were you struggling to push out of your head? When you were thought-less, what did you experience?

The Accomplishments Within You

When we think of accomplishments, we tend to look outside of ourselves.
Instead consider accomplishments that have occurred within you?

Where have you grown? How have you overcome adversity? Resisted temptation? Embraced positive change?

What have you discovered? Create a list of some of your internal achievements.

And Now What?

Rabbi Adin Steinsaltz has said that the most important Jewish question is: "And now what?"

You may have answered, "Is there a God?" but "now what?" You may have gotten married but "now what?" What are you to do with your convictions?

We often become complacent once we find answers and solutions. How will you live a life of shared values that raises you both up higher? Where can you continue to strive further by asking the next level "and now what?"

Relationships

People You Love

Who are people you love who make you better when you are around them?

How can you more deeply cultivate these relationships?

Community Part I

In what ways are you struggling to connect to community? In what ways do you feel fulfilled and connected to some community?

What are you looking for and not finding?

How can you give more to a community? How can you connect more deeply with a community that you value?

Teachers and Mentors

Who are some of your greatest past teachers and mentors? What made them impactful for you?

Who are some of your current teachers and mentors? Are they right for you? If so, how can you cultivate your precious experiences with them more deeply? If not, how can you find the right teachers and mentors for you?

Are there people that *you* can help teach and mentor?

Students and Teachers

Greatness cannot be measured by who your teachers were, but by who your students are.

Who are you empowering to be their greatest?

What talent are you supporting today? What makes them good students? What makes you the right teacher?

Friendship

What are some of the friendships that you would like to invest more deeply in?
What are some of the past friendships that you need to move on from or let go?

In what aspects are you seeking new partners and friends in your life?

How will you go about finding them? How can you be a better friend to those you care about?

Trust

A recent Pew study found that the Millennials (those between 18-33) are "distrustful of people." Only 19 percent of Millennials say that most people can be trusted. There is certainly no virtue to be naïve or indiscriminately trusting, but there is a virtue to be a trusting person (one who can appropriately and maturely trust others who deserve that trust). A safe and sophisticated society requires a culture of trust and interdependence.

Where do you struggle with trust?

How might you experiment with being more trusting?

Toxic Forces

Unfortunately, there are times in life when we encounter people who bring us down through their actions. It could be friends, old and new or, sadly, significant others.

Who are some of those people and what are some of the situations in your life that have been toxic, destroying your inner joy and spirituality?

How can you move away from these people and situations where possible or have difficult conversations when necessary?

Fear of Social Alienation

Jewish law teaches that when one has a bad dream about being ostracized that one should find 10 people to help release them from that ban (*Hilchot Talmud Torah* 6:12). We all feel, in different ways, fear of social alienation and estrangement.

When do you feel socially alienated? How does the fear of being more isolated affect you? How might you address this?

Community Part II

It is not rare that individuals become disillusioned with (and even quit) their community because a policy is created on which one strongly disagree. But a community is not one's family room where one should love and agree with everything and everyone. The whole idea of a community is that each person must pull himself or herself back to appreciate the majority of experiences and ideas that work for them while creating space for things that work for others.

Ideally, we give more than we take in community. Where can you be less critical of a community that you're in that is creating a space that is meaningful for others (even if it does not work for you)?

Jews and Gentiles

Rabbi Ahron Soloveichik wrote:

> "From the standpoint of the Torah, there can be no distinction between one human being and another on the basis of race or color. Any discrimination shown to a human being on account of the color of his or her skin constitutes loathsome barbarity. It must be conceded that the Torah recognizes a distinction between a Jew and a non-Jew. This distinction, however, is not based upon race, origin, or color, but rather upon *kedushah*, the holiness endowed by having been given and having accepted the Torah. Furthermore, the distinction between Jew and non-Jew does not involve any concept of inferiority but is based primarily upon the unique and special burdens that are incumbent upon the Jews" (*Logic of the Heart, Logic of the Mind*, 61):

He makes clear that all humans are equal, yet we all have different tasks. Jews have unique demands based upon our special moral charge and destiny.

In what ways do you feel most broadly human? In what ways do you feel distinctly Jewish?

How might you strengthen each of these attributes of your identity: integrated within humanity and also unique and special because of tradition and culture?

Role Models

Who are some of your role models of the past? What did you learn from them?

Who are some of your role models today? What are you looking to learn from them and how can you best achieve that?

How are you serving as a role model for others?

Healing

Regret

Where do you feel some pain, guilt and/or regret in your life?

How can you address this past situation and continue to heal?

Try to sustain the difficult return to these feelings.

Self-Care Part II

What are you doing to take care of yourself?

What are some new things you can do to make sure you are ensuring balance, positivity, and healthful living in your life?

Wronged

Who has hurt you?

How can you continue to heal from this pain? How can you continue along a path of forgiveness?

Physical Health

How are you taking care of your body (diet, exercise, healing) on a daily basis?

What else can you take on to enhance daily living?

Fear

What are you afraid of that you wish to overcome? Make a list.

How is each of those fears preventing you from actualizing your potential? How can you overcome (or productively channel) these fears?

Prayer and Ritual

__Prayer__

Prayer comes naturally for some and with much more difficulty for others. Some have simple and pure faith and some have always struggled to believe. Some connect with traditional liturgy while others need to use their own words.

What is your personal prayer practice?

Cultivating the Soul

What if we were all to take just one minute a day to meditate (with all of our energy) on the beautiful spark of illuminated holiness within our souls?

We have trouble carving out the time for the most important work sometimes. I think the biggest struggle many have is not believing in their soul, but picturing it in a concrete way. So I think we first need to learn to discover a concrete image of our soul. That image should not only be personal and authentic but also should fill one with joy and love when focused on it. Once we find it, we just need to hold the image in our mind (and heart) for as long as we can. As one grows with experience, one can potentially ditch the concrete image and move toward the metaphysical realm.

Some moments, we may need to retreat or hide in our souls when in fear or pain. Other times, we need to fly into our soul to expand ourselves in search and exploration. It's about engaging both immanence (the metaphysical theory of divine presence) and transcendence. First, we need to access it, know it, own it, love it, and cultivate it. This eternal part of us is the essence of our existence and the most precious diamond we will ever discover.

Write about how you experience your soul. Draw an image that to comes to mind.

Singing

Professor Ron Heifetz said: "I think we build religious institutions to give people a safe place to sing."

Have you found a safe place for yourself where you can sing with others and feel interconnected harmony? What does that feel like for you?

"Features of the Jewish Tradition"

Albert Einstein said, "The pursuit of knowledge for its own sake, an almost fanatical love of justice and the desire for personal independence – these are the features of the Jewish tradition which makes me thank my starts I belong to it."

How do you embrace these ideals within a Jewish context?

- Pursuit of wisdom?

- Pursuit of justice?

- Pursuit of personal drive and sustainability?

Reverence for Creation

Susan Neiman wrote:

> The attempt to tame reverence into doctrines and practices is as precarious as it is natural. One moving effort to shape reverence is the intuition of the Sabbath. Jewish traditions understands the commandment *remember the Sabbath day and keep it holy* as a demand to show reverence for Creation. If God rested on the seventh day to contemplate the goodness of His work, we ought to follow Him by reminding ourselves that life itself is more important than all the business with which we usually fill it up (*Moral Clarity*, 243-44)."

How might you utilize the Sabbath to increase your reverence for creation?

Conversion

The Jewish community is very open to accepting converts. These individuals who bravely embrace Judaism without having been raised Jewish are to be considered heroes and role models in the community. Jewish law demands that they are cherished, embraced and never shunned.

After completing Jewish learning courses, committing to Judaism and the Jewish people, dipping in the *mikvah* (spiritual bath) and getting circumcised (for boys), converts are celebrated in the community and are no longer consider "converts" but just normal Jews.

What does this conversion mean to you? How can this new beginning serve as a re-birth for you? (or how might you embrace this new convert in a new more special way)?

Journeying

Preparing for a Trip

What are you most excited for on this voyage?

What are you feeling anxious about?

What are you trying to get out of this experience?

End of a Life Journey or Stage

What was particularly difficult for you on this journey? How will you process this and grow from this?

How will you protect yourself from this?

What was particularly meaningful for you on this journey? How will you continue to connect to this? What did you come to learn about yourself and what you want and need?

Legacy

What do you want for your life legacy? How do you want to be remembered?

What would you want said of you at your funeral?

If you were so inclined, what song(s) would you like played at your funeral?
Further, if there were one sentence about your life written on your tombstone, what would it say?

Retirement

What aspects of retirement will be challenging for you? How can you mitigate this challenge?

What aspects will be liberating? What are some new life goals for yourself that you have in this new exciting stage?

Growth

__Freedom__

What's an area of your life where you're looking for freedom (physical, emotional, or spiritual)?

Who will your partners be in helping you get there?

Obstacles

What are some obstacles in your life that are preventing you from being your best?

How can you overcome these obstacles? Who are your partners and supporters?

Argument

Rabbi David Hartman once said: "Weakness invites aggression; strength invites a moral argument."

How are you at embracing challenge?

Are there some relationships (or contexts) where you tend to act defensively where you might be able to listen and engage more deeply?

Your Well

In the Torah when we learn that Miriam passes away, we immediately learn that there was no more water for the Israelites to drink. The commentators taught us that Miriam's gift was ensuring water for the people and so when she ceased, water ceased.

There seems to be a suggestion inherent in this that we each have special gifts to offer – take a few minutes now to reflect on and write about what your gift might be – something that you can provide uniquely in the world (suggestion – do not be intimidated by the comparison to Miriam – begin by thinking about what you already offer to family and friends). Maybe your gift is already clear to you, maybe it is still emerging – feel free to explore, to imagine what will emerge as your special gift.

Measuring Success

How do you measure success in your life?

What are your core values and goals that you bring into your daily assessment of personal success?

Struggle

The essence of the Jewish people is struggle. This was why Jacob's name was changed to "Israel" because Israel means, "to struggle with God."

How can you embrace struggle and tension with more productive discomfort? How can struggle elevate you rather than slow you down?

Blinders

There is an old phrase: "To the blind all things are sudden."

We often feel startled because something happens that we did not expect but we should have expected.

Where are some of your blinders today?

Is it possible for you to slow down and heighten your other senses when something blinds you?

Moral Inconsistency

We all live with moral inconsistency. Consider, for example, how philosopher Jean-Jacques Rousseau wrote one of the most seminal works on raising children to be independent and free citizens, while leaving his own children in an orphanage.

Where are some of the hypocrisies in your own life where you live in a way different than you believe and maybe even preach? Try to be really honest with yourself. And then if/when you're ready consider some baby steps to put your beliefs and teachings into practice on the next level.

Getting Back Up

King Solomon taught: "A righteous person falls down seven times and gets up," (Proverbs 24:16). Life is constantly testing us.

How can you use some recent challenges/failures/struggles to help you become stronger, healthier, and more prepared to fulfill your life mission with joy?

Theory of Behavioral Modification

What is your theory of behavioral modification?

How do you work to change a personal behavior that is deeply ingrained in you?

What partners and systems of accountability could you put in place?

Vision

What is your vision for your life in 5 years? 10 years? 20 years?

What activities can you put into each day to help ensure that you are proactively working towards achieving those visions?

__Momentum__

Often we have momentum in our day and there are obstacles (whether people or situations) that break our concentration or groove.

What are some of your momentum-breakers?

How can you prevent these from blocking your moments of actualization when you're in the zone personally or professionally?

Sacrifice

What would you be willing to sacrifice to help others? What discomfort would you embrace to enhance the dignity of another? What would it take for you to reduce some pleasure to help another fulfill their needs?

Life Curriculum

Take some time and create your own learning curriculum.

What are the all the things you want to learn over the course of your life?

When will you learn them?

Which topics can wait 5-10 or 10-20 years and which do you really want to tackle *this* year?

How will you structure your time?

Who and what will you learn from?

Daily Tasks To Improve

Pick one thing in your life that you're not happy with and that you want to improve.

Now make a list of 3-5 small daily tasks that you can do to improve in that area. They should be small and nothing so major that they will become a significant burden with your time and energy.

Striving for Excellence

Pick one area of your life that you want to strive for a higher level of excellence?

How can you increase your performance? What kind of investment would it take?

What kind of partnership and support would you need to get there?

How can you cultivate the resilience to do the hard work to get there?

Reflecting on the Past

Learning Moments

Reflecting upon your journey, what have been some of your most important life learning moments?

How can you continue to learn from them?

Traumas and Glories

What have been the defining traumas and glories in your life?

How might they be connected (if it all)?

Childhood

Think about your most powerful and memorable childhood experiences. Write about 3 of your best and 3 of your most painful.

What is it about them that has stuck with you?

How and why are they still with you and a part of you?

Nostalgia

Memory is powerful at individual and collective levels. We weave together special life moments to create a cohesive nostalgic whole; it's where we go to seek refuge into happiness and comfort.

Yet, nostalgia can also trick and hurt us. It can project false perceptions on the past and make the present and future too distant for us to function.

Where does your nostalgia give you warmth and strength? Where might it hold you back?

Yichus

In an age where one judged their value by their ancestry, Rabbi Yechiel M'Ostovtze wrote: "*Yichus* (noble ancestry) is similar to a bunch of zeroes. They don't have any meaning unless there's a real number at the beginning." Our lineage only has value if we live a life that honors it. We are not great because of where we came from but because of what we achieve with that privilege.

In what ways are you proud of where you came from? In what ways, can you seek to differentiate yourself and become your own unique self?

Ethical Dilemmas

What was a recent ethical dilemma you had? How was it resolved?

What is your process to resolve the ethical dilemmas you encounter? How can you strengthen your process to ensure you are as intentional, thoughtful, and deliberate in this process as possible?

Morning Blessings

Day and Night

"Blessed are You, Hashem, our God, King of the universe, Who gave the heart understanding to distinguish between day and night."

The human capacity for reflection and reason is truly miraculous. Who can you embrace this blessing more deeply?

Sight to the Blind

"Blessed are You, Hashem, our God, King of the universe, Who gives sight to the blind."

Each of us has "blind spots." How can you gently and productively help another see their blind spots?

Clothes the Naked

"Blessed are You, Hashem, our God, King of the universe, Who clothes the naked."

What are the "clothes" that you choose to wear in your life? How do you express yourself publicly? Why do you express yourself in that way? How is shame and dignity connected to how you dress and present yourself?

Releases The Bound

"Blessed are You, Hashem, our God, King of the universe, Who releases the bound."

Where are you stuck in your own life? Where are you looking for freedom?

How will you get there?

Strengthens the Bent

"Blessed are You, Hashem, our God, King of the universe, Who straightens the bent."

Each day, we are given the gift of life. It is a vote of confidence in our existence. We rise from our beds and embark upon our life mission. How can this daily occurrence of getting out of bed be ritualized to cultivate gratitude? With a song? Prayer? Meditation perhaps?

Strength to the Weary

"Blessed are You, Hashem, our God, King of the universe, Who gives strength to the weary."

Where do you need more strength in your life? How will you get it? How are you strengthening others?

Gives Knowledge

"Blessed are You, Hashem, our God, King of the universe, Who has given of His knowledge to human beings."

What is the unique knowledge you have and cherish? How can you share that knowledge with others? In what areas are you looking to become more knowledgeable?

Ethics of the Fathers

The World Stands on Three Things

1:2 – "Shimon the Righteous was among the last surviving members of the Great assembly. He would say: The world stands on three things: Torah, the service of God, and deeds of kindness."

How are you embracing these three in your life: Torah (learning and growth), God (spiritual searching and connecting), and kindness (giving)?

In what ways can you grow in each?

Motivation

1:3 – "Antignos of Socho received the tradition from Shimon the Righteous. He would say: Do not be as slaves, who serve their master for the sake of reward. Rather, be as slaves who serve their master not for the sake of reward. And the fear of Heaven should be upon you."

While Judaism is concerned with actions and outcomes, there is also a significant concern about the inner life.
What drives you?

How are you cultivating positive intentions and motives?

Sages

1:4 – "Yossi the son of Yoezer of Tzreidah would say: Let your home be a meeting place for the wise; sit in the dust of their feet, and drink thirstily of their words."

How do you open your home to others? How do you make your home a place of learning?

How can you surround yourself with people of virtue and learning?

Relationships

1:6 – "Joshua the son of Perachia would say: Assume for yourself a teacher, acquire for yourself a friend, and judge every person to the side of merit."

Who are 2-3 of your teachers and mentors today? Who are 2-3 of your friends you can rely on deeply?

How can you strengthen those relationships and internalize their teachings more deeply? How can you give more to them?

How do you judge others unfairly? How could you curb that desire?

Peace

1:12 – "Hillel would say: Be of the disciples of Aaron – a lover of peace, a pursuer of peace, one who loves the creatures and draws them close to Torah."

How do you pursue inner peace? What spiritual practices do you have to achieve this?

How do you pursue external peace? What types of conflict do you look to assist in ending or mitigating?

Myself and Others

1:14 - "[Hillel] would also say: If I am not for myself, who is for me? And if I am only for myself, what am I? And if not now, when?"

How can you engage in more care ensuring that you protect yourself? On the flip side, how can you engage more sacrifice to leave your personal comfort zone to give more to others?

Greeting Others

1:15 – "Shammai would say: Make your Torah study a permanent fixture of your life. Say little and do much. And receive every person with a pleasant countenance."

How do you greet others? How can you add more joy and warmth to how you greet those you love as well as strangers?

Law, Truth and Peace

1:18 – "Rabbi Shimon the son of Gamliel would say: By three things is the world sustained: law, truth and peace."

What do you do to help foster the strength of law, truth, and peace in your home? In your community? In society? Where could you do more?

Community Part III

2:5 – "Hillel would say: Do not separate yourself from the community. Do not believe in yourself until the day you die. Do not judge your fellow until you have stood in his place."

We need community to stay humble and empathic.

What barriers do you have in your life to being consistently present, participatory, and giving?

How can you become more humble in your communal involvement and embrace opportunities to learn about others' challenges and struggles?

Study

2:5 – "And do not say 'When I free myself of my concerns, I will study," for perhaps you will never free yourself.'"

What enables you to procrastinate your intellectual enrichment and personal growth?

How can you take time out of your "too busy" schedule to prioritize your own development?

Good Traits

2:13 – "[Rabbi Yochanan] said to them: Go and see which is the best trait for a person to acquire. Said Rabbi Eliezer: A good eye. Said Rabbi Joshua: A good friend. Said Rabbi Yossei: A good neighbor. Said Rabbi Shimon: To see what is born [out of ones actions]. Said Rabbi Elazar: A good heart."

How can you cultivate each of these traits of being:

- A good eye -

- A good friend -

- A good neighbor -

- A good anticipator -

- A good heart -

Overcoming Negativity

2:16 – "Rabbi Joshua would say: An evil eye, the evil inclination, and the hatred of one's fellows, drive a person from the world."

Where are you being defeated through negativity, anger or hatred? How can you shut those channels off or redirect those energies?

Property of Others

2:17 – "Rabbi Yossei would say: The property of your fellow should be as precious to you as your own."

Do you find yourself being more reckless with property that is not yours, but is perhaps public property, your employer's property, or a friend's property? How can you show the same level of care (and maybe even more) that you show to your own?

Work

2:20 – "Rabbi Tarfon would say: The day is short, the work is much, the workers
are lazy, the reward is great, and the Master is pressing."

What is the real "work" you do in the world? How can you fit more of your life purpose into your daily routine?

Resiliency

2:21 – "[Rabbi Tarfon] would also say: It is not incumbent upon you to finish the task, but neither are you free to absolve yourself from it."

Some tasks we never take on and some causes we never support because we cynically believe that we are not capable of change. Jewish wisdom teaches us that we may not refrain from engagement just because we are not capable of creating the ultimate change ourselves.

What issues have you been afraid of engaging because they seem too daunting?

How can you take some baby steps forward to engage in causes that are meaningful to you?

Fear of Doing Wrong

3:11 – "Rabbi Chanina the son of Dosa would say: One whose fear of sin takes precedence to his wisdom, his wisdom endures. But one whose wisdom takes precedence to his fear of sin, his wisdom does not endure."

Ethical virtues *must* precede intellectual wisdom. That wisdom will not be sustained or actualized if it does not have a strong ethical foundation.

How do you cultivate the fear of doing wrong?

Deeds Before Wisdom

3.12 – "[Rabbi Chanina, the son of Dosa] would also say: One whose deeds exceed his wisdom, his wisdom endures. But one whose wisdom exceeds his deeds, his wisdom does not endure."

One of the greatest ways we learn about ourselves, others, and life is by doing. How can you put more of your truths into practice?

Supporting Leaders

3:16 – "Rabbi Ishmael would say: Be yielding to a leader, pleasant to the young, and receive every person cheerfully."

How do you support leaders who need public support? How do you serve as a gentle mentor to others looking to grow?

Humility

4:4 – "Rabbi Levitas of Yavneh would say: Be very, very humble, for the hope of mortal man is worms."

What does humility mean to you? What thought experiment (viewing one's mortality, for example) inspires humility in you?

Afterlife

4:21-22 – "Rabbi Yaakov would say: This world is comparable to the antechamber before the World to Come. Prepare yourself in the antechamber, so that you may enter the banquet hall… He would also say: A single moment of repentance and good deeds in this world is greater than all of the World to Come. And a single moment of bliss in the World to Come is greater than all of the present world."

How do you prepare yourself for the afterlife? What if you were to view this life as a preparatory room in anticipation of "real" existence?

Beyond the Surface

4:27 – "Said Rabbi Meir: Look not at the vessel, but at what it contains. There are new vessels that are filled with old wine, and old vessels that do not even contain new wine."

How can we get beyond surface reality? What experiments could you try to see beyond the surface level of realities you encounter?

Rechanneling Energy

4:28 – "Rabbi Elazar HaKapor would say: Envy, lust and honor drive a person from the world."

How do these three vices manifest themselves in your life? How can you remove their potency and re-channel the desires?

Temperaments

5:13 – "There are four types of temperaments. One who is easily angered and easily appeased – his virtue cancels his flaw. One whom it is difficult to anger and difficult to appease – his flaw cancels his virtue. One whom it is difficult to anger and is easily appeased, is a *Chassid* (a righteous/pious person). One who is easily angered and is difficult to appease is wicked."

What triggers anger in your life? How can you ensure that those stimuli don't work to cause a rise in you? How can you pull yourself from anger more quickly?

Learning and Filtering

5:18 – "There are four types among those who sit before the sages: the sponge, the funnel, the strainer and the sieve. The sponge absorbs all. The funnel takes in at one end and lets it out the other. The strainer rejects the wine and retains the sediment. The sieve rejects the coarse flour and retains the fine flour."

How do you detect and reject harmful ideas you encounter? When reading books, watching movies, and engaging in conversation, how do you ensure that you do not internalize the messages that you feel are immoral and untrue while still embracing other concomitant ideas that seem true and virtuous?

Love

5:19 – "Any love that is dependent on something – when the thing ceases, the love also ceases. But a love that is not dependent on anything never ceases."

Think about those you love most. What do you expect from them? What would it look like to love them without demands and expectations?

Disputes

5:20 – "Any dispute that is for the sake of Heaven will have a constructive outcome; one that is not for the sake of Heaven will not have a constructive outcome."

Analyze the last 3-5 arguments you had. What was motivating you in each of them? Do you find yourself arguing from a place of ego or playing "devil's advocate?" How do you ensure that your arguments are motivated by a desire for relationship strength, truth, and virtue?

Inspirational Quotes

Great Transformations

Carl Jung once wrote: "In the last analysis, the essential thing is the life of the individual. This alone makes history, here alone do the great transformations take place, and the whole future, the whole history of the world, ultimately springs as a gigantic summation from these hidden sources in individuals."

It is inside of you where the great drama of life occurs.

What is the great transformation (revolution of the soul) you are embarking upon?

Paradox

Walt Whitman once wrote: "I contradict myself. I am large. I contain multitudes." When we embrace the complexity of life, we come to accept that we live in paradox. We cannot resolve all of our tensions or big questions.

What are some of the big paradoxes and contradictions you're sitting with?

How can you become more okay with this?

__Become a Self__

Nietzsche once wrote: "Active, successful natures act, not according to the dictum 'know thyself,' but as if there hovered before them the commandment: will a self and thou shalt become a self."

How are you actively constructing your "self?"

What can you do daily to create your very being?

I Control My Life

James Allen wrote: "[Y]ou are the maker of your thought, the molder of your character, and the maker and shaper of your condition, environment, and destiny."

How can you gain more confidence to embrace control of your life?

Our Thoughts

Ralph Waldo Emerson wrote: "A person is what he thinks about all day long."

Where do most of your thoughts go? To work? Fears? Daily tasks? How can you reclaim part of your mind to re-define yourself based upon where you take your mind?

Solitude

Blaise Pascal said: "All man's miseries derive from not being able to sit quietly in a room alone." There is credence in the notion that much can be heard and discovered in quiet solitude.

Where are you finding time and space to be alone, reflect, and listen to yourself?

<u>Boundaries</u>

In his poem *Mending Wall,* Robert Frost wrote: "Good fences make good neighbors."

How might you create boundaries to protect your own dignity?

Do you adequately protect yourself?

Do others ever take advantage of you in any ways?

Transitions

Ralph Waldo Emerson wrote: "Not in his goals but in his transitions man is great."

How do you transition between major events in your life?

Consider a few transitions you made.

What worked well and what did not? What felt right and what did not? What transitions do you have coming up and how can you plan differently for them based upon your learning here?

Wasting Your Spiritual Capital

American psychotherapist and author Richard Carlson once wrote: "So many people spend so much of their life energy 'sweating the small stuff' that they completely lose touch with the magic and beauty of life. When you commit to working towards this goal you will find that you have far more energy to be kinder and gentler."

Where are you spending too much emotional and spiritual energy on little things that are not most important for you and are unlikely to matter a year from now?

How can you shift from these concerns that are draining your spiritual potential?

Concern for Others

Dale Carnegie wrote: "Remember that the people you are talking to are a hundred times more interested in themselves and their wants and problems than they are in you and your problems. A person's toothache means more to that person than a famine in China which kills a million people. A boil on one's neck interests one more than forty earthquakes in Africa. Think of that the next time you start a conversation."

While it's an unpleasant reality, we know how true it is that humans are necessarily (albeit tragically) self-absorbed.

What would it look like to take one step in the other direction?

To listen a little more intently and empathically? To subdue a bit more of your own personal concerns in front of another's greater welfare?

The Law of Giving

Deepak Chopra wrote:

> "The best way to put the Law of Giving into operation…is to make a decision that at any time you come into contact with anyone, you will give them something. It doesn't have to be in the form of material things; it could be a flower, a compliment, or a prayer… The gifts of caring, attention, affection, appreciation, and love are some of the most precious gifts you can give, and they don't cost you anything" (*The Seven Spiritual Laws of Success*).

Try this experiment for a day or a week. What is one thing you could leave everyone you talk with (physical, verbal, or emotional)?

Flow

Hungarian-American psychology professor Mihaly Csikszentmihalyi, in his book *Flow,* writes about the importance of engaging in optimal experiences (the aforementioned "flow").

What types of experiences do you immerse yourself in and feel a deep sense of connectedness and meaning?

How can you expand this flow beyond those moments?

Spiritual Being

French philosopher Pierre Teilhard de Chardin, SJ wrote: "We are not human beings having a spiritual experience, we are spiritual beings having a human experience."

Our essence is indeed spiritual but too often we silence that to exist in the pragmatic realm on a surface level.

How can you develop your spiritual side so that it emerges in all that you do?
(This is about changing how you "be" in the world, not what you "do.")

Going Inward

Henry David Thoreau wrote: "All men plume themselves on the improvement of society, and no man improves."

Thoreau observed that many blame politicians, human nature, and society for their challenges rather than taking responsibility.

While there is infinite work to do to improve the world outside of us, we must also be working on ourselves. Write about two aspects of yourself you'd like to work on this month.

<u>Meaning</u>

Viktor Frankl, a psychoanalyst and a Holocaust survivor, observed that those who survived the horrors of the concentration camps most often had one thing in common. They were not physically stronger, more religious, or smarter. They were able to construct meaning in their life. He argued that the determining foundation of humans is the ability to make our own meaning of our existence.

How do you actively make meaning out of your highs and lows in life?

What is your process to interpret your life situations in a way that gives you clarity and purpose?

Emotional Intelligence

American psychologist Daniel Goleman writes: "Emotional life is a domain that, as surely as math or reading, can be handled with greater or lesser skill, and requires its unique set of competencies. And how adept a person is at those is crucial to understanding why one person thrives in life while another, of equal intellect, dead-ends: emotional aptitude is a meta-ability, determining how well we can use whatever other skills we have, including raw intellect."

What are a few aspects of your emotional life that tend to confuse you, get you in trouble, or prevent you from actualization?

Pick 2-3 and explore how you might develop your emotional intelligence more deeply on them.

Habits of the Mind

William James suggested: "Genius…means little more than the faculty of perceiving in an [non-habitual] way." Where have your thought patterns and spiritual approaches become so habitual that you're no longer seeing and feeling anew?

Further, Lao Tzu wrote: "Be still, and allow the mud to settle. Remain still, until is the time to act." There is an art to timing, like the martial arts.

What experiments can you try to clear your mind?

What is something sensitive coming up in your life that you can think very carefully about your timing for action?

Our Grand Spectacle

Victor Hugo wrote in *Les Misérables*: "There is one spectacle grander than the sea, that is the sky; there is one spectacle grander than the sky, that is the interior of the soul."

An encounter with a starry night or a wavy ocean can strike deep awe and wonder in all of us.

How can an encounter with your soul (an "event of the soul") strike even grander insight in you while on a walk, lying in bed, or in meditation?

Responsible for Oneself

M. Scott Peck wrote: "Once you admit that 'life is difficult,' the fact is no longer of great consequence. Once you accept responsibility, you can make better life choices."

What is one significant life choice you have coming up where you can accept full responsibility for how you respond?

Raise Your Standards

Motivational speaker Tony Robbins wrote:

> "Any time you sincerely want to make a change, the first thing you must do is raise your standards. When people ask me what really changed my life eight years ago, I tell them that absolutely the most important thing was changing what I demanded of myself. I wrote down all the things I would no longer accept in my life, all the things I would no longer tolerate, and all the things that I aspired to becoming."

Where can you demand more of yourself?

Are there aspects of your life that mean so much to you that you can try to raise the bar to a higher level of excellence?

Going Out To The Woods

Henry David Thoreau wrote in *Walden*: "I went to the woods because I wished to live deliberately, to front only the essential facts of life, and see if I could not learn what it had to teach, and not, when I came to die, discover that I had not lived."

In certain environments we can all think more clearly. How can you go out to the "woods?"

Is there a special place you can go to from time to time where you can re-gather yourself and find clarity?

Building Castles In The Sky

Thoreau wrote: "If you have built castles in the air, your work need not be lost; that is where they should be. Now put the foundations under them."

We should never stop dreaming. It is essential in life to think big and dream high. If we wish to actualize those dreams, we need to bring them down to earth. Write about one life dream you have and how you can help to transition it from the heavens down to earth.

How You Make Others Feel

Maya Angelou once said: "I've learned that people will forget what you said, people will forget what you did, but people will never forget how you made them feel."

Our speech and actions are so important. Additionally, the way we impact others with that speech and action is crucial.

How do you think others feel after interactions with you? More tired, frustrated, or negative? Or uplifted, empowered, and loved?

How can you experiment with focusing on your own speech and actions but also really accounting for how others are feeling when with you?

Meditation and Writing

Fun

It's important to find enjoyment in life.

How can you add more joy into your daily living? How can you add more fun things into your life that give you strength and joy?

Who are people you have responsible fun with and how can you engage them more?

Each Moment

We are given 86,400 gifts every day. This is the number of seconds that God gives us each day to live life to our fullest. Take a few moments to meditate on the seconds as they pass by.

How can you appreciate and embrace these seconds more deeply?

Standing Up

Rabbi Abraham Joshua Heschel once said: "To be is to stand for!" This quote suggests that we gain our existence by standing up for our core values and convictions.

What do you stand up for publicly, loudly, and proudly?

How can you embrace your existence through your commitment to your highest ideals of kindness, love, and justice?

Wearing Our Own Clothes

Before battle, David was given King Saul's armor. This is certainly fitting for him since he is to become a king as well. But David tries on the armor and takes it off; it is not him. He knows that to go to war, he must be himself.

For each of us this is true too. When we go to battle, as it were, in the world, we must wear our own clothes.

What are your clothes that you wear to go out and be your most unique self?

Peace Through Conflict

Rav Kook asks a question on the verse: "Sages increase peace in the world." Rav Kook asks how this can be since the primary function of the Talmud is to engage in intellectual and spiritual argument and debate. He explains that the deepest and most enduring peace is one that has a foundation of argument.

This is true for us as well. In our precious relationships, we should never argue unfairly but we should share feelings of disagreement in order to get to deeper levels of truth and love. It is through productive conflict that we can build true, enduring, and loving peace.

How do you engage conflict in your own relationships? Do you sometimes fight unfairly making personal attacks?

How can you be more courageous to bring important issues to surface and also more gentle, humble, and loving in how you share and listen within that intention? Do you sometimes avoid important issues because you're risk averse?

Ethical Will

Many leave money for their children as an inheritance after they pass. This is a kind gift if one is able to do so. However, even more meaningful, is the practice to leave an ethical will (one's core teachings, values, experiences, and dreams – words of love and blessing).

If you have not yet, begin to write your first ideas of what you'd like to include in your ethical will. None of us know when we will pass from this world but we should always be prepared to live each moment as if it may be our last.

Meditation

Try experimenting with a new type of meditation you have not done before: mantra (repetition spoken out loud), a visual contemplation (with a candle, flower, picture, or some still object), a sound meditation (waves breaking, chirping crickets, or a violin), a smell meditation (a fragrance or spice) or a touch-based meditation based.

Write about how these experiments affect you. What books can you read? What teacher can you go to improve your meditation experiences?

Mental States

There are two types of spiritual experiences: hot spirituality and cold spirituality. In the *hot* mode, it's like being in the library on fire with ideas; the mind is totally on. In the *cold* mode, it's like laying on a beach or in a cold shower; the mind is relaxed.

Think and write about how you engage in these two types of mental states and how you transition between them. Which works better for you?

Channeling Emotions

The Hasidic masters taught that rather than destroy unhealthy emotions, one should channel them.

What is an emotion that is leading you astray from your true self that you can channel that energy toward something healthy and productive?

Divine Chariot

The Book of Ezekiel describes a Divine chariot (*maasei merkava*) that is made of many angels. It is a prophetic vision of God surrounded by heavenly creatures.

These angels (and the Divine presence) are present in our lives. How can you start to see them with you? Write about the attributes of strength, compassion, and healing and how you want to surround yourself with those virtues.

Hitbodedut and *Hitbonenut*

Rebbe Nachman of Breslov taught a unique approach to *Hitbodedut* (self-seclusion): he suggested that one shouts inside of one's own head. One is not actually screaming, however, only screaming in their brain.

Try this when you're alone and able to dedicate a few minutes to intensely focus.

Now write. What did you hear when you started screaming as loud as you could?

Self-Understanding

Try growing in your *hitbonenut* (self-understanding) by being *medabair l'atzmi* (talking to yourself) in the past or future. Mediate on your childhood self and talk to him/her. Meditate on an older you.

Have conversations with each of them.

What do you learn about your past, current, future fears, perceptions, hopes, and dreams?

Writing A Prayer

Write your ideal prayer, one that you can recite daily when you wake up or before sleep. It should include your hopes, request, gratitude and wishes. Use your own voice.

There is no correct personal prayer. It should just be true to your heart.

Wonder

Consider this quote by Rabbi Abraham Joshua Heschel from *Man Is Not Alone*:

> Among the many things that religious tradition holds in store for us is a legacy of wonder. Wonder goes beyond knowledge. Wonder is a state of mind in which we do not look at reality through the perspective of our memorized knowledge; in which nothing is taken for granted…. As civilization advances, the sense of wonder almost necessarily declines. Such decline is an alarming symptom of our state of mind. Mankind will not perish for want of information; but only for want of appreciation. … What we lack is not a will to believe but a will to wonder… Wonder is not the same as curiosity. Wonder is a form of thinking. Wonder, rather than doubt, is the root of all knowledge. There is no answer in the world to radical amazement.

How do you engage wonder? What spaces can you create in your life for curiosity and exploration?

Missing the Burning Bush

The commentators suggest that Moshe missed the burning bush at first. He just did not see it. Ramban explains that this is because "Moses didn't see the presence because he hadn't prepared his heart for prophecy" (Exodus 3:2).

What is the burning bush in your life that you are not seeing yet?

In what ways can you prepare your heart so that you can see the remarkable messages you are intended to receive at the right moments?

Standing Before The Divine

Set an alarm for 5 minutes. Make sure you're alone, stand up straight, be silent, close your eyes, and imagine that you are standing directly in front of the Divine.

What is this experience like for you? What did you feel?

Write about this encounter.

Your Inner Light

Close your eyes and focus all of your energy upon your inner light.

Now right about this experience.

What does your light look and feel like?

How does it nourish you? How can you bring it with you in your journeys?

Sefirot

Research the meaning of the ten Kabbalistic *sephirot*:

- *Keter* – crown
- *Chochmah* – wisdom
- *Binah* – understanding
- *Chesed* – kindness
- *Gevurah* – strength
- *Tiferet* – beauty
- *Netzach* – eternity
- *Hod* – splendor
- *Yesod* – foundation
- *Malchut* – kingship

Explore how you can develop a connection (a channel above) through each of these ten attributes.

Holidays

Rosh Hashanah

The Jewish New Year provides a special opportunity to make changes in our life direction.

What are 2-3 new commitments you can make in your life to improve yourself this year? What are 2-3 old commitments you can let go of that are no longer fulfilling or no longer have enough significance in your life?

Yom Kippur

Who do you need to ask for forgiveness this year?

How can you prepare for this conversation? How can this conversation strengthen the relationship if it's important to you or help you let go of the relationship if it's better to be over?

Who is someone that you can continue to try to forgive in your heart?

Sukkot

Sukkot is a time to remember that our possessions are fleeting. We cannot take them with us when we pass from this world.

What are some ways that you have become too attached to materialism and physical possessions?

How can you take one step further in de-emphasizing their significance in your life? How can you connect more on this holiday with the nature, others you cherish, with God, and with yourself?

Simchat Torah

How can you cultivate more joy in your relationship to Jewish learning and values? How can you live your values with full rigor, but add an element of joy into your deepest life commitments as well?

Chanukah

Where are you receiving light in your life? How can you strengthen the opportunities that give you wisdom, motivation, inspiration, and joy?

Where are you putting light out in the world? How can you strengthen these opportunities to ensure that your talents and gifts are being actualized to inspire and support others?

Tu B'Shevat

How do you feel connected to nature? How can you deepen your connection to the earth and sky? How can you receive energy and equanimity from the environment around you?

Have you considered stargazing, gardening, hiking, or the like?

Purim

In the Purim *Megillah,* Queen Esther finds herself in a unique position inside the palace to make a real difference for her people.

Where do you have power? Where can you use your position of influence to make a difference in/for your community?

Passover

The Hebrew word for Passover is *Pesach*. The Kedushat Levi says *Peh-Sach* is about using speech to speak about God and the good. He contrasts this with *Paroah* (Pharoah) who is *Peh-Raah* (bad mouth) and uses speech to diminish, harm, and destroy. The Torah teaches that we should elevate our mouths to make music, build others up, and spread light.

Do you tend to gossip, spread rumors, or speak badly about others behind their back? How can you take a step forward to minimize that? How can you use speech more positively to build up, encourage, and inspire others?

Counting the Omer

The Omer is what connects Pesach to Shavuot, thus connecting the intersection between liberation and actualization, collective narrative and individual journey, and natural law with Divine law. We need to take what we know from experience and intuition (*yetziat mitzryim*) and codify it into law (Shavuot). Counting the Omer, for me, is an act of solidifying this bond between what we know and what we must do. It's a move from epistemological and ontological reality to pragmatic and normative necessity.

It's a practical mitzvah that is about counting each day, appreciating each moment, and keeping track of our growth. Create a 49-step plan for something you want to work on in your life. Count each day of the Omer and track your daily growth over the 7 weeks to monitor your development on this task.

1.)

2.)

3.)

4.)

5.)

6.)

7.)

8.)

9.)

10.)

11.)

12.)

13.)

14.)

15.)

16.)

17.)

18.)

19.)

20.)

21.)

22.)

23.)

24.)

25.)

26.)

27.)

28.)

29.)

30.)

31.)

32.)

33.)

34.)

35.)

36.)

37.)

38.)

39.)

40.)

41.)

42.)

43.)

44.)

45.)

46.)

47.)

48.)

49.)

Yom HaShoah

How do you personally connect and experience Holocaust Remembrance Day?

What feelings emerge for you? How does your own unique memory lead to your own unique action/response?

Yom Ha'Atzmaut

What does Israel Independence Day mean to you?

How can you connect more deeply to Israel in the coming year?

In what ways might you explore supporting our Jewish democratic state?

Lag B'Omer

The *Zohar* says that on the day when Rabbi Shimon died, his home was filled with *Aish Kodesh* (the fire of holiness), and a heavenly voice burst forth announcing an invitation to bring his righteous soul to the heavens. The fire that filled Rabbi Shimon's home is symbolic of the Kabbalah, the esoteric, holy, mystical wisdom of the Torah.

How can you embrace more of the awe and mystery of existence? What's the unique *aish kodesh* (holy fire) inside of you?

Shavuot

On this holy day of revelation, what type of discovery are you yearning for?

How can you get closer to understanding the truth you are so hungry for?

Tisha B'Av

On Tisha B'Av, we experience our brokenness and the brokenness of the world.
Yet, we yearn for repair.

What is something of the past that you have lost that you yearn to return to, but know you cannot?

How do you make that value manifest in the world today?

Where have you experienced destruction where you must continue to rebuild?

Shabbat

How can you improve your Shabbat experience making it more separate from the other six days of your week?

What could you do to make it even more joyful, spiritual, reflective, and meaningful?

Who are some others you could grow your Shabbat practice with (in learning, prayer, walking, meals, etc.)?

Minor Fast Days

On this fast day, how can you use this break from food to return to food differently?

How can you eat in a more healthy way? How can your meals be more socially uplifting? How can the food you eat be in line with your moral and spiritual values?

Conclusion

Now that you have completed these writing exercises, consider and write about these questions:

Where has this writing journey taken you so far?

What has the experience of going back to read your writing from this last year been like for you?

What have you learned about yourself?

How will you continue your writing?

Were there 5-10 specific writing prompts that worked for you that you might return to write about again in the future?

Closing Thoughts

Rabbi Avraham Yitzchak HaCohen Kook, the first Chief Rabbi of pre-state Israel, once said: "I don't speak because I have the power to speak; I speak because I don't have the power to remain silent."

I would extend this to writing as well. We may not think we have the power to write but the truth is that we don't have the power not to write. Our soul is craving exploration and discovery. We don't have the power to silence its melodies or to dim its light.

All we can do is search, explore, and discovery.

All we can do is write.

Illustrations:

Front & Back Cover – "Cirrus Clouds in late afternoon, over Warsaw, Poland." Uploaded May 22, 2005. Photo by Przemyslaw Idzkiewicz. This file is licensed under the Creative Commons Attribution-Share Alike 2.0 Generic license. Author does not specifically endorse use of this photo.

Daily Living – "Nostalgia Train Returns" by Metropolitan Transportation Authority of the State of New York uploaded by tm. This file is licensed under the Creative Commons Attribution 2.0 Generic license. **Public Domain** Image

Joyful Occasions – "Running with the Seagulls – Galveston, Texas" by Ed Schipul. 3 December 2006. This file is licensed under the Creative Commons Attribution-Share Alike 2.0 Generic license. **Public Domain** Image.

Loss - "Sunset" – 2006 by Nevit Dilmen - GNU Free Documentation License; This file is licensed under the Creative Commons Attribution-Share Alike 3.0 Unported license. **Public Domain** Image.

Social Change - "Civil Rights March" - This photograph is a work for hire created between 1952 and 1986 by one of the following staff photographers at *U.S. News & World Report*:

Warren K. Leffler (WKL)
Thomas J. O'Halloran (TOH)
Marion S. Trikosko (MST)
John Bledsoe (JTB)
Chick Harrity (CWH)

It is part of a collection donated to the Library of Congress. Per the deed of gift, *U.S. News & World Report* dedicated to **the public all rights it held for the photographs** in this collection upon its donation to the Library. Thus, there are no known restrictions on the usage of this photograph."

Social Justice – "Young Protester Screaming" by Heng Reaksmey. Uploaded 25 October 2013
This media is in the **public domain** because it is material provided by Voice of America, the official external radio and TV broadcasting service of the U.S. Federal Government.

Middot and *Mitzvot* – **Public Domain** Image. Author unknown. Upload date unknown.

Virtues - Detail from "The School of Athens" by Raphael. This is a faithful photographic reproduction of a two-dimensional, **public domain work of art**. The work of art itself is in the public domain for the following reason: This work is in the public domain in the United States, and those countries with a copyright term of life of the author plus 100 years or less. Currently located at the Apostolic Palace, Vatican City.

Leadership – "Conductor Justin W. Lewis leads a joint concert of Air Force Band musicians and music students from the College of William and Mary." [No date] Uploaded by LoneCello This file is licensed under the Creative Commons Attribution-Share Alike 3.0 Unported license. **Public Domain** Image.

Imagination – "Thomas Lorenzo on Acoustic Guitar" - uploaded by Fgil65 on October 13 2003 .I, [Fgil65] the copyright holder of this work, release this work into the **public domain**. This applies worldwide. In some countries this may not be legally possible. if so:
I grant anyone the right to use this work for any purpose, without any conditions, unless such conditions are required by law.

Happiness and Spirituality – "Silhouette and Sunset in Fuvahmulah, Maldives" by Nattu [July 25, 2007]. This file is licensed under the Creative Commons Attribution 2.0 Generic license. Public Domain Image.

Relationships – "Friends" 26 January 2012 Author Vaibhav Sharan. This file is licensed under the Creative Commons Attribution 2.0 Generic license. Public Domain Image

Healing – "Young and Old Hands" by Øyvind Holmstad 8 May 2011. This file is licensed under the Creative Commons Attribution-Share Alike 3.0 Unported license. Public Domain Image.

Prayer and Ritual – "Shabbat Candle" by Olaf Herfurth. 6 March 2010. This file is licensed under the Creative Commons Attribution-Share Alike 3.0 Unported license. Public Domain Image.

Journeying - (NPS Photo/Kent Miller) "McKinley and a Hiker" 28 July, 2009 Creative Commons Attribution 2.0 Generic license. **Public Domain Image**.

Growth – "Sailors Climb Obstacle Course Rope" by US Navy. 11 September 2012. This file is a work of a sailor or employee of the U.S. Navy, taken or made as part of that person's official duties. As a work of the U.S. Federal Government, the image is in the **public domain**.

Reflecting on the Past – "Una Señora descansa en la Plaza Colonial de Parita" by Pastor Morales. 31 August 2013. This file is licensed under the Creative Commons Attribution-Share Alike 3.0 Unported license. **Public Domain** Image.

Morning Blessings – "Water Lily" by John Sullivan. Uploaded 2-28-2013 by Fae. This work has been released into the **public domain** by its author, Jon Sullivan. This applies worldwide.

Ethics of the Fathers – "Jewish Children with their Teacher in Samarkand (Cropped)." An early color photograph from Russia, created by Sergei Mikhailovich Prokudin-Gorskii as part of his work to document the Russian Empire from 1909 to 1915. Part of the Sergei Mikhailovich Prokudin-Gorskii Collection (Library of Congress). **Public domain.** This work is in the public domain in Russia according to article 1256 of the Civil Code of the Russian Federation.

Inspirational Quotes – "Rosa 'Inspiration' in the Rosarium Baden in the Doblhoffpark in Baden bei Wien." Identified by sign. 6 June 2014 by Anna reg Permission is granted to copy, distribute and/or modify this document under the terms of the GNU Free Documentation License, Version 1.2 or any later version published by the Free Software Foundation; with no Invariant Sections, no Front-Cover Texts, and no Back-Cover Texts. A copy of the license is included in the section entitled GNU Free Documentation License. This file is licensed under the Creative Commons Attribution-Share Alike 3.0 Austria license. **Pubic Domain** Image.

Writing and Meditation – "A Kid Writing or Drawing " by dotmatchbox at flickr. 25 February 2011. This file is licensed under the Creative Commons Attribution-Share Alike 2.0 Generic license. Public Domain Image.

Holidays – "Passover Seder Dinner at the White House 2011" by Pete Souza. United States President Barack Obama and First Lady Michelle Obama mark the beginning of Passover with a Seder on 18 April 2011. The diners are seated on Chiavari chairs in the Old Family Dining Room of the White House. This work is in the **public domain** in the United States because it is a work prepared by an officer or employee of the United States Government as part of that person's official duties under the terms of Title 17, Chapter 1, Section 105 of the US Code. [Note: the inclusion of this picture by the author does not indicate or forward a political position. It is a fascinating image of a sitting President of the United States partaking in one of the most ancient Jewish rituals. This warrants its inclusion in the book].

Rabbi Dr. Shmuly Yanklowitz is the Executive Director of the Valley Beit Midrash, Founder and President of Uri L'Tzedek, and Founder and CEO of The Shamayim V'Aretz Institute. He completed his Master's at Yeshiva University in Jewish Philosophy, a Master's at Harvard University in Moral Psychology and a Doctorate at Columbia University in Epistemology and Moral Development. Rav Shmuly is the author of six books on Jewish ethics, theology and philosophy. *Newsweek* listed Rabbi Yanklowitz as one of America's Top 50 Rabbis.

Made in the USA
San Bernardino, CA
09 May 2017